A JOURNEY TOWARDS SUSTAINABILITY?

BOOK 1 'HICCUPS AND ALL'

Stella Evelyne Tesha

authorHOUSE®

AuthorHouse™ UK
1663 Liberty Drive
Bloomington, IN 47403 USA
www.authorhouse.co.uk
Phone: 0800 047 8203 (Domestic TFN)
+44 1908 723714 (International)

Published by AuthorHouse 10/17/2019

ISBN: 978-1-7283-9474-9 (sc)
ISBN: 978-1-7283-9473-2 (e)

Print information available on the last page.

Contents

Foreword

At first I only thought of focusing on sustainability and environmental poems, mainly because my mind is usually occupied by sustainability issues; Why do they exist? What is the easiest way to make people understand? Who should be involved? How should anyone be involved? How do we solve them collectively?

Being knowledgeable and passionate about sustainable development and environmental management has been both a blessing and a curse for me. A blessing because I have come to understand many of the issues especially how the social, politics, economics and environment are inseparable and interrelated. A curse because I do not have the opportunities or the power I need to be able to make a real difference and therefore it makes me frustrated.

Anyway.... along the way I got distracted by political issues which are currently happening around the world but most specifically in Tanzania. It became impossible to separate sustainability, environmental management and the politics. Instead of giving in to frustration, I decided to follow through knowing that everything happens for a reason. I wanted to share the reality of my journey with you therefore I ended up producing two books instead of one as planned. Book two focuses on the journey towards sustainability *'Politricks and Polipricks'*.

Acknowledgements

I have only been able to write these poems because of my academic background in social sciences, politics and governance, international development, environmental policies, project management, sustainable development and environmental management. For this I truly thank my various professors and supporting academicians from the Open University of UK (Milton Keynes).

I also want to thank all my children for always and enthusiastically expressing their flattering and unflattering opinions about my work. Their perspectives are important and have given me insight as well as the motivation I needed to complete my work despite the many distractions.

I appreciate my parents, my sisters, my brothers, my aunts and uncles for contributing to whom I have become.

Many thanks to my dear friends who are my soul sisters and brothers because their diverse ways of thinking usually validates the right for everyone to be different and have helped me to grow as a person.

Last but not least, I would like to thank the true hero of my heart. Finding each other again have been the best gift from God.

There is always something to learn.
We must keep learning every day from everything and from each other.
Only then can we become our true selves......

1 - The Journey Towards Sustainability

The Journey towards sustainability,
is but a journey to improve ability,
ability to survive in harmony,
ability to preserve what is,
ability to improve chances for continuity,
ability to become better,
better within our environment,
better within ourselves.

Then came globalization,
with that, expansion,
expansion of boundaries,
which triggered competition,
and that in turn triggered exploitation,
and eventually, structural oppression,
that, has been the journey so far,
making sustainability bizarre.

Yet, the answer is but simple,
sustainability is within us,
within our inner selves,
a state of self we can achieve,
the best answers are never external,
not only from policies,
not only from technology,
but by making a conscious inner choice ...

To journey towards sustainability.

2 - What About The Next Generation?

What about the next generation?
what price will they pay?
what about globalization?
what about free trade?
what about monoculture?
what about genetic modification?
what about hydroelectric dams?
what about wind farm projects?
what about resource mining projects?
yes, what about those?

We continue the 'good' fight,
naturally..............
it is what we learnt after all,
the heaviness of the pockets,
that is termed as success,
in this age of business competition,
much comparable to hunting grounds,
in this age of improved hunting,
civilised contracts negotiations,
you take that market, I take this,

Plundering of resources,
profit making,
multilateral agreements,
inventions of new technology,
implementations of land projects,
the 'pricing' of pollution,
innovations for adaptability,
exhilarating international meetings,
sustainability we call it,
development...............

To whom does it matter?
who collects the gains?
yes, who?
who are the losers?
where do they go?
do they live to see the day?
is this systematic extinction?
well, is it?
can you be sure it is not?
can you?

What about the next generation?

3 - Maybe It Is That Age...?

Yes, maybe it is that age?
a mother says that a lot,
"maybe it is that age"
the age for unexplained tantrums,
the age of endless questions,
the rebellious age of a teenager,
till recently termed as most destructive.

So maybe it is that age,
that which is most destructive,
the age of clearing forests for monoculture,
the age of extreme resource plundering,
the age of commercializing industrial pollution,
the age when wars are business ventures,
a most prosperous age for the two faced.

Maybe it is that age....???

4 - I Can Not Breath!

Atchooooo! Aaaaaatchoo!
'I cannot breath' the young one says,
breathing in and out with difficulty,
'oh dear! The dust! The smog!
it makes me itch, it gives me allergy,
mama! The young one weakly calls,
endless silence is all there is,
'mama?' The young one asks fearfully,
as she gently sways,
feeling, learning,
all senses reaching out,
maaamaaaa! she screams,
at the sight she now beholds,
the mothers rapidly dying,
some burnt out before the act,
some chopped in multiple pieces,
the lonely tree, a heart breaking fate

5 - Nature Displacement

From the eyes of the Orangutan,

We used to call this home,
now we have nowhere to go,
it matters not that we are intelligent,
or that we use their human tools,
if evolution takes it's course,
before we go extinct,
we may even attend schools,
and maybe get white collar jobs,

We sleep in nests, so what?
humans used to sleep in caves,
look where they are now,
the monsters of our nightmares,
sure we forage for food,
some planted by them humans,
is this reason to terminate our race?
after taking our homes, our livelihoods?

Sigh! relocation is a must,
although no place seems safe,
they fear us, as we fear them,
we run, they kill,
sure we have two great options,
life imprisonment or death,
it is doom for the man of the forest,
nature displacement,

From the eyes of the orangutan.

6 - Humans As The Face Of Evil

In the animal kingdom,
evil wears the face of human....

We the human species,
regarding ourselves as superior,
have destroyed animal habitats,
have killed their brothers and sisters,
have chained them in enslavement,
have poked and pricked for experiments,
have stolen their horns and skins,
have eaten their meat excessively,
billions of races single handedly destroyed,
now climate change accelerated by humans,
depriving them of natural habitats,
destroying the food chain,
do you wonder what they teach their young?
if they have the chance that is ....
animal history lesson 1 - human greed and exploitation
animal History lesson 2 - enslavement by human
animal History lesson 3 - experiments done by human
animal History lesson 4 – families destruction by
humans
humans, as the natural enemies,
that is the foundation of all the lessons,
is this flattering you of the human race?
the race you see as superior?

In the animal kingdom,
evil wears the face of human.........

7 - A Painful Death

It felt as if she's being strangled,
as her throat closed tighter and tighter,
the burning never ceased,
as she gasped for breath,
'how much longer must I endure?',
painful thoughts crosses her mind,
she struggles to move forward,
gasping for breath, chocking,
in her head screaming for help,
help that never came.

With every breath inhaling chemicals, oils,
there is no place to escape,
no place to hide,
as the end came to their world,
who does such evil things?,
sadness overcomes her,
as she realises her fate,
final tears,
adding to salt in the sea,
as mama fish draws her last breath,

Her struggles stop.................she rests in peace.

8 - Extinction

Climate and ecosystem are changing,
altering vegetation,
destroying natural food sources,
disrupting birth schedules,
exposing animals to unusual climate,
some may yet adapt,
many may not,

Hyper diseases, a climate change impact,
destroying the mega-fauna,
causing drastic species extinction,
in a space of few centuries,
two thirds of large mammals population,
gone,
by the end of ice age.................................

Looking back centuries ago,
eating, barter trade, the reasons for hunting,
hunting methods simple and effective,
guns, is what we have now,
mass murder, for profit reasons,
complete extinction,
delayed by policies and restrictions,

Many species fall victims,
to this wonderful industrial era,
creation of roads through wildlife habitats,
oil spills in the high seas,
chemical wastes dumped in the oceans,
air pollution from industries.,
an everyday occurrence,

Changing climate,
destroying ecosystems,
altering vegetation,
eliminating food sources,
disrupting birth schedules,
extinction, of vulnerable species,
some may adapt......

9 - Another Whale Tale

Another whale tale,
right now,
the largest mammal on the planet,
there used to be others....
like the woolly mammoth,
no longer in existence,
it happens.....

Another whale tale,
food becoming scarce in the high seas,
dumped chemicals damaging my lungs,
so much waste I can not digest,
the same problem for cousin dolphin,
as sea temperatures continue rising,
breeding becomes more impossible......

Another whale tale,
ocean acidification,
stripping carbonate ions from seawater,
young eggs birthed with weak shells,
for lack of calcium carbonate,
our skeletons become weaker,
our breed is doomed for extinction,

Another whale tale,
like all extinction before,
the human race, are at fault...............

10 - Green Gold

'Biofuels' they call it,
green energy, green gold.....
or a cover for something else?
perhaps mass logging?
palm oils, liquid gold,
a reason for monoculture,
deforestation, destruction,
mass murder of species,
land pollution,
water pollution,
air pollution,
in the end of it all,
a remote controlled economy,
as the price rests on demand,

Monoculture economy?
what a risk!
a cure for poverty they say,
environmental sustainability,
what about the biodiversity loss?
the source of many medicines,
once a wide range of free selection,
now all needs to be imported,
or manufactured,
a cure for poverty?
hell no!
just another gold rush,
another threat, to the ecosystem.

'Biofuels' they call it,
green energy, green gold....

11 - The Environment Price Tag

Clean drinking water?
"sorry dear, we can't afford it",

Once upon a time that used to be free,
we would walk along the road,
and pick up pretty colored pebbles,
collecting piles of them,
even building tiny doll houses,
behind our backyards......
now there is a price tag on pebbles,
it does sound ridiculous,
since just 20 years ago,
it used to be free!

Yes, the water also,
it used to be free,
we would just dip our bottles,
in clean rain water pools,
or the lakes, or natural springs,
that used to flow along,
they are no longer of course,
evaporated from climate change,
now we buy in bottles,
with a 'spring water' label.
I sometimes wonder,
if there were past events,
which made some stones so rare,
maybe 1,000,000 years ago,
gold could be found on the streets,
only there were no streets,
maybe diamonds were found in water,
the dry lands of now not then,

and maybe rubies are hardened skeletons,
of some long ago creatures.

Now nothing is free,
except the air we breathe,
it won't surprise me one day,
if oxygen masks become a must,
backpack oxygen bottles to be refueled,
and for those who can't afford,
life expectancy will be short,
lungs inhaling industrial fumes,
slowly burning to crisps,
a torturous death indeed!

Clean drinking water?
"sorry dear, we can't afford it"

12 - Dodo's Last Flight

Like any other day,
her feathers blown by the wind,
varied shades of white and black,
a large swollen looking beak,
defense against nature's breed,
dreaming of savory fish, seeds and fruit,
reminiscing of her young age,
plump and pretty she was,
with but short wings,
not made to fly afar,
and now, a rushed flight,
aiming for the edge of the cliff,
breathless...
sharp eyes evaluating the landing,
on the last safe place.... she thinks,
maneuvering the infant on her back,
her old bones as weary as her mind,
she carefully puts down the little one,
the last one of her kind,
'be brave my child' She says,
in you, we might be reborn,
that was the dodo's last flight

13 - The Displaced Gene

The displaced gene,
what we call a GMO,
genetic manipulated organisms,
the man made world,
the stranger gene,
what are you doing here?
where do you want to go?
how will you grow?
how many will you destroy?
how will you break the food chain?

The displaced gene,
are you just the displaced gene?
or the future biodiversity?
and you my dear 'original' friend,
who will soon be displaced,
the critical natural resource,
for the displaced gene,
now gracing the land you stand,
feeding on the bacteria beneath your feet,
clueless of the coming future....

The displaced gene,
would you also depend on bacteria?
to break down nutrients for you,
so that you can absorb and grow,
no? what is it I hear you say?
you are the assassin of all pests?
beetles, fungi, bacteria alike?
it wasn't the original intention?
but you soon took over?
and became the pest-terminator?

The displaced gene,
the new pest terminator,
even the valuable ones,
the planet life support,
you were invited, you say?
to cure the world from poverty,
to 'end' the hunger,
who then owns you?
are you free for poor farmers?

The displaced gene,
this is I!
where do I want to go, you ask?
everywhere, my job is to take over,
how many will I destroy, you ask?
I am still exploring potential,
mutating, reproducing, fearsome descendants.........
you may want to watch your back,
when and how we populate,
it could go either way......

The displaced gene,
take a look at me!
how will I break the foodweb, you ask?
in so many ways you see!
I will kill the soil bacteria,
so your original plants can't feed,
sweet extinction of plant lives!
grazing animal will soon go hungry,
carnivorous will fight to feed,
and all along I'll grow stronger,

The displaced gene,
many bodies shall die and rot,
providing more beasts to kill,

deeper entrenchment of my roots,
ain't that the sweetest deal?
in the end, I, will, be, 'the',original,
my masters shall be my slaves,
to live and die at my will!
their diet depending on me!
I, the displaced gene...........

14 - Hail To The Environment!

Hail to the environment!
you are a worthy warrior,
whatever we do to you,
you manage to fight back,
eventually we lose off course,
you are like a bank account,
debit and credit reconciling,
or consequences are faced,

Hail to the environment!
the way you handle pollution,
the more we send to the atmosphere,
you send back a reminder,
worsening climate change impacts,
floods, tornados, hurricanes,
we can learn to swim of course,
but what of draught and forest fires?

Hail to the environment!
the way you handle big projects,
big dam projects do not daunt you,
we can get the electricity of course,
but the diversion caused by projects,
leaves less fish for consumption,
dead vegetations behind reserves?
deadly organic poisonous weapons!

Hail to you environment!
you must certainly be amused,
gazing at round table discussions,
listening to the broadly discussed 'issue',
'environment sustainability',

of course we agree,
on that one 'concept' at least,
the rest is pay check time,

Hail to the environment!
as continue to fight our differences,
on what's important to do,
which policies to write,
what are priority issues,
and you listen so patiently,
o! environment,
the master of all outcomes,

Hail to you environment!
I hail you once more,
and I take my hat off,
until we meet again,
until we encounter your wrath,
would it end from greenhouse gasses?
or shall it be volcanic eruptions?
is the end in our hands?

Hail to the environment!

15 - The Brain And Evolution

The brain and evolution,
a curse or a blessing?

Evolution,
the ongoing process of life,
earth life as it has always been,
questions of the brain and evolution,
brain cells replicating, dividing,
as any other organic cells,
these must keep dividing,
as they reach the growth extent,
that support the cytoplasm.

Why then do brain cells divide?
is it due to the food we eat?
or maybe from information absorption?
does that lead to evolution?
from proto humans to homo sapiens?
or does it lead to extinction?
can we tell from lab experimentation?

If information cause brain modification,
and such change is the outside reflection,
what of this era of abundant information?
if the food we eat cause the modification,
and we go along with GMO consumption,
will there be consequences exemption?
and is there time to take precaution?

The brain and evolution,
a curse or a blessing?

16 - Poor Environment!

Poor environment!
what have you ever done,
to deserve this fate?

You provide us with all,
food, shelter, luxurious goods,
all served on a silver platter.

We want more than you can give,
all knowledge created with this perception,
we drill, plough, heave and shift,
making you our personal gift,

The more we get,
the more we want,
with better technology,
comes greater destruction,

Technology, the tool for destruction,
simplification of economic exploitation,
magnification of environmental destruction.

17 - Biodiversity Or A Lab Creation?

What is nature, what is not?

Biodiversity or a lab accident?
what is nature and what is not?
the new viruses that can't be cured,
an experiment gone wrong or evolution?

Visualize a superb scientist,
with time for nothing but science,
no wife or kids to yell stop!!! off course,
or 'what the plum are you doing!!!?'

He puts the pet rat in a techno-cylinder,
mixed with genes of god knows what!
forgetting to turn it off, and days go by,
the rat's brain evolves like yours did!

The tail grows, shrinks, drops off,
scientists works, snoozes and dozes off,
the techno-cylinder eventually switches off,
the super rat-human then steps off,
biodiversity or a lab accident?

Biodiversity and change go hand in hand,
change of climate, change of vegetation,
extinction followed by mutation on new species,
could mythical creatures have been biodiversity?
or a lab creation of some past?

What is nature, what is not?

18 - Once Upon A Time

We will start with 'once upon a time'
and continue with 'a long long time ago!'
'.. it was the Phanezoic era,
fruits were in abundance,
so many varieties in taste, shapes, genes,
even scientists couldn't categorize them all!
have you ever heard of the Papayas?
those orange fleshy sweet fruits?
mostly common along tropical zones,
yes indeed there were geographical zones!
even reliable climate patterns,
ah! for the taste of a kiwi fruit!
once also known as 'the vitamin bomb',
now known as the 'amazing Ki-nut'
a bio combination with some nut,
there used to be a variety of nuts,
now we have what is called a Fu-nut,
a nuts fusion achieved in some lab,
we had cows, goats & sheep,
now known as the 'Cogosh' breed!
to conserve the environment they say,
why diversity while you can have one?
they eat too much green! they said,
spinach, cabbage and broccoli,
now the advertised hero vegetable 'scabro',
sustainability by gene-fusion,
this is where we are now,
it has been a long journey,
from biodiversity to bio-uniformity,
the world we have today,
made from our yesterdays,
once upon a time................

19 - The Capitalist Concept

The capitalist concept as I see it,
accumulating wealth for the sake of wealth,
every morning the same old fate,
waking up early to start the day,
raising tense with expectations,
a strained string ready to snap,
rushing through traffic,
trying to beat deadlines,
day in, day out,
like the robots and modern machines,
those of which we have created,
our currency for efforts made?
we must earn the "daily" bread,
how much bread can we consume?
bigger houses, fancier cars?
more shoes, like Madonna?
we work, day in, day out,
saving for fancy "vocations",
none like the previous years,
one such as Trump will take,?
the capitalist concept as I see it,
accumulating empty wealth,
collecting debts,
"needs' increasing with each pay check,
with every extra penny we earn,
spend! spend! spend!
haven't you seen the amazing discounts?
spend! spend! spend!
black friday sales?
spend! spend! spend!
what of halloween? christmas? easter?
not to forget birthdays and thanks giving?

spend! spend! spend!
work! work! work!
spend! spend! spend!
work! work! work!
impossible to stop,
temptation is the master,
spend! spend! spend!
work! work! work!

The capitalist concept as I see it,
we are after all the slaves of it,
it all seems so natural,
"a way of life" if you please!
no brains left to question,
evolution stopped somewhere,
no previous history in the gene pool maybe?
no past lessons learnt?
we submit to the polluting system,
like elegant resigned zombies,
the brain numbing existence,
high end designer clothes,
status set by the car you drive,
this is what we call progress,
energy spent in wealth accumulation,
empty wealth we hardly need,
what strange beings we must seem!
and some work makes no sense,
like lying politicians for example,
a highly paid job, an empty profession,

So beautiful, so seductive,
so humbling and truly majestic,
the capitalist concept as I see it.

20 - The Frog's Message

The man sat down under the tree,
dozing off in his favorite garden chair,
the frog hopped on his foot, nudged him,
and looked up at him beseechingly,
'if only I was a man' the frog thought,'
'I heard that!' man said,
'you did? well ..... I still think it!' said frog,
'why-ever would you want to be a man? 'asked man,

'Well, man can do interesting things, said frog,
they can walk to anywhere,
and when it is a long journey,
they can take a fancy ride,
they can change any situation,
to fit what they feel is best,
they can eat everything,
they can live in nice houses,
and when there's rain or sunshine,
they never seem to get affected, 'said frog.

'That's all you know of men!' man responded,
we fight and creatively steal,
we hate and work endlessly,
as if that's not enough,
we always seem to want more,
the world destruction is by men,
we see ourselves as mini gods!
we struggle daily to maintain the farce,
you wish you were a man?
gosh! I wish I were a frog!,' said man.

'So did I', said frog,
and hopped away ....

21 - Huh!! What Next??

Collective action you say?
environmental sustainability?
clean development mechanism?
fair trade? free trade?
the words may mean something,
to some, like a red flag to a bull!

I don't understand my leaders,
nor the named " international" world,
always using big words,
throwing them around like corns,
expecting all to jump and catch,
and do a bidding accordingly.

I am a born and bred villager,
living from hand to mouth,
I worry not about the environment,
as long as it feeds my family,
nor do I care for collective action,
I long more for shelters and clothes.

Don't Speak to me of fair trade,
where is this fairness you talk of?
do you take time to analyze the costs?
not from your point of view, but mine?
if fair trade is really fair,
how come you get rich and I don't?

Free trade! another laughable concept,
another word for modern imperialism,
these signed modern treaties by 'leaders',
good for their growing stomachs,

the rich continue to feed,
like leeches!
the poor go on to perish,

Were there free trade conditions?
when the west first fought to protect their markets?
how fair is the concept of fair trade,
when some have subsidies and some don't?
how can you expect collective action?
with such inequalities and diverse priorities?

I understand the 'hype' of the west,
especially when it comes to free trade,
it's all about national interests,
which every country should do,
I just don't understand our leaders,
not trying to promote the same!

Huh!! What next??

22 - Depth And Breadth In Life

Any life force has depth and breadth,
if it wasn't for that no life will survive,
have a look at the trees for a live example,
as they grow their roots bury deeper,
could you pause and think, why that is?
this is nature, the nature of life,
as we grow older, we are meant to dig deeper,
deep in our souls, in our minds,
every minute, every hour,
take the wisdom from a baobab tree,
"pretty flowers and shiny leaves,
will not sustain it from giant storm",
just as a wise woman will say,
"seems to me pretty flowers and shiny leaves,
have much in common with,
pretty makeup and shiny shoes",

That is just one angle of it of course,
I've also been aware of life's course,
we give up too much control,
to those whom we term superior,
those may be individuals nearby,
or some far reaching fingers,
governance institutions, company structures,
the economy situation, social influences,
all those and other agents,
influencing development in depth and breadth,
breadth seems to be the trend,
more work, more purchases, bigger houses,
expenses, stress, manipulations,
all are part of a network of this current life,

we accept this development of life in breadth,
with much help from external agents,

Why do we need bigger houses?
why do we need the latest phone?
why do we need expensive cars?
why do we thrive for power?
why do we fight for the highest salary?
why do we invade our neighbors?
why do we refuse to reduce pollutions?
why do we buy brands and trends?
we do all that and more,
because we grow in breadth,
we forget to dig deeper,
as the wise baobab tree taught us,
pretty flowers and shiny leaves,
will not sustain us from the coming storms.

23 - A Somber Thought

I look back to the days of freedom,
the times of visiting my grandparents,
such freedom we had,
running through nature, wild and untamed,
feeling as one with the birds on trees,
no care, no worries,
the sun shining on my bare head,
feet covered in dust and bruises,
climbing trees as nimbly as monkeys,
eating those mangoes, pears and nuts,
drinking water from mountain springs,
a real holiday feeling!
every day, each day,
from sunrise to sun set,
enjoying every fruit flavor,
as picked straight from the tree,
juices dripping down the chin,
what a joyful mess!
real happiness for my belly,
sugar canes, like unlimited candy,
many a tooth ache that gave me,
my grandma would then remind me,
to put some clove in my tea,
that kept tooth pain away,
and ginger tea twice a day,
always kept the colds away,
my grandma was one of the wise,
the wisdom learnt from environment,
growing up from the village,
every each piece of nature offers a lesson,
the many different types of soils,
possess qualities for growing different crops,

the many leaves, fruits, and roots,
being remedies for different aches and pains.
fresh honey from the bees,
a soothing cure for cuts and burns,
the great wilderness is now gone,
replaced by neat rows of coffee or corn,
how much corn can one eat?
no more fruits to pick and choose,
the birds left, seeking food and new homes,
how I miss the mornings filled with birds chorus!
nature has become a rare quality,
no more bees to offer free honey,
they need food too to stay alive,
most animals have left the grounds,
we now purchase what was once free,
slowly all nature become undone,
all that thrives are coffee and corn,
economic development we call it,
for the price of life..........
human life, nature's life,

What a somber thought this is!

24 - Remembering Natural Development

Remembering......
the many past educational holidays,
sitting on my grandpa's feet,
him telling tales of great feats,
tales to learn from,
with moral guidance till today,
'a story is not just a story', he would say,
in the end always ask yourself,
'what does the story mean'
'what has the story taught me'

The lost opportunities of yesterday,
the teachings of wise elders,
now children would watch TV,
or listen to MP3's all day long,
there is quite a lot of information,
the brain has no time to process,
no time to ask the two important questions,
sadly no moral lessons to lead the young,
and most information is misguiding,
most parents unaware............

Remembering......
the many past educational holidays,
sitting on my grandpa's feet,
him telling tales of great feats,
tales to learn from,
with moral guidance till today,
'a story is not just a story', he would say,
in the end always ask yourself,

'what does the story mean'
'what has the story taught me'

This is where we are now.......
elders roles made obsolete,
TV, MP3, ipads........ now play that role,
no feeling of continuity for the young,
no feeling of worth for the old,
no stories of surviving local disasters,
no stories of those who fought for justice,
no stories of plants curing dementia,
no stories of conflicts being resolved,
where do we go from here?

Remembering natural development......
'what does the story mean'
'what has the story taught me'
my grandfather would ask,
he would expect a real response,
my grandfather, he was wise,
as his father before him,
and his son after him,
this story means much is lost,
the story teaches we must re-learn,

..... And teach

25 - Envisioning The End

Envisioning the end....
natural air suffocating and heavy,
thunderous clouds tramples through localities,
darkened skies from unusual activity,
screams ringing through the stinging air,
howls of terror mingle with the cracking of trees,
unnatural thunder rampages the forest,
various inhabitants gripped with fear,
heartbreaks,
frantic searches for lost siblings,
skulls cracking from felling trees,
until all is gone,
no more trees to shelter and nurture,
contribution to biodiversity extinction,
erosion, waste,
all washed to seas and oceans,
stilts, chemicals, claiming more lives,
yet, all it takes is 5 seconds,
to tear through a gift paper,
the paper that cause so much devastation,
or the detached term called deforestation.

26 - The Last Man Standing

Rivers, mountains, sunshine, rain,
all that has not been made by man,
wildlife, glaciers, land and crops,
all that is necessary for man existence,

Demise ....
tornados, spawned by violent storms,
harmless objects turn into missiles,
heat waves, persistently burning crops and flesh,
weakening living organisms to the breath,
flooding, landslides and sea level rise,
causing deaths and property destruction,
desertification, the ghost of former flourishing lands,
now unable to sustain the tiniest life,
wildfires, tearing like a stampede through forests,
a barbeque banquet fit for the mother,
or perhaps a favorite wife,

The unstoppable power of nature..........
sweeping through planet earth,
as the ultimate vacuum cleaner,
wiping out the human race,

The last man standing,
with conflicting emotions,
defiantly resigns,
to the wrath of climate change.

27 - The Tattered Old Man

Yes, I could tell you a story that will open your eyes,
though that depends on the openness of your minds.

I, the tattered helpless old man,
kicked around on the streets,
treated as nothingness,
was once a proud king!

Yes young man, I too have a history,
gene by gene, we transferred to our young,
much as your ancestors persist to remain blind,
playing oblivious to their crimes,

I, once a proud grandfather of many generations,
spreading my seed throughout nations,
helped by insects, birds, wind, and water, birds,
within a harmony that existed,

The great forests are no longer.
a home for many, a home no more.
disharmony caused by humans,
gone, my home, my family, why!!!?

Now I am blown around your filthy streets,
reduced into despicable litter,
hoping for recycle to retain my gene,
or a merciful death, to end the pain.

I, once the grand king of the forests!
from beautiful green to dustbin.

28 - So What?

Life as it is, is filled with wonders,
wonder we haven't yet perceived,
wonders we may never perceive,
we have kept boundaries of the mind,
isn't it possible a musician can also be other?
look at Will Adams, a great pop artists,
and yet, an IT innovator,
look at Chris Rock, a hilarious comedian,
yet, also a politician,
look at honey, a tea sweetener,
but also a healing agent,
look at the sun, the moon, the ocean,
imagine the wonders held by nature,
all to be revealed at it's own time.

Nature, a complicated concept,
do we understand nature?
do we understand it as the lion does?
or do we understand it as a fungus does?
what about the vegetables?
are they not too part of nature?
do we then not all...
have different understandings?
different perspectives?
so what?
so what if a woman loves a woman?
so what if a man loves a man?
so what if a one wants to be one or another?
is love not better than hate?

I look at the children murdered in Gaza,
I look at the many meaningless wars,

I look at leaders justifying the wars,
I look at leaders initiating wars,
I look at flourishing weapons industries,
and I sigh!, exhausted in the meaningless world,
a world more comfortable with war,
tolerant to Donald Trump,
yet shuddering at the thought of same sex love,
people, I don't mean to call you names,
I have quite a selected few,
do we really think we own the rights,
to decide how one should live, or not?
who are you?

Yesterday, he saved your child from being hit by a car,
yesterday, he put out a fire at your neighbor's house,
yesterday, with an operation she saved your loved one's
life,
yesterday, she won a marathon for the country,
you call them heroes, you deny them human rights,
what kind of hypocrisy is that?
love, is everywhere, in many forms,
love, frowned upon, as we accept war,
we deny them rights,
the very rights we claim for ourselves,
why?
tell me dear imbeciles of today,
is it better if the child you love today.
is raped in the future to come?

That is the choice you are offering,
for generations to come,
if one is forced to be with one,
not the one she or he would rather be with,
that is indeed the definition of rape,
the other option is to be alone,

you wonder about the statistics of failed marriages,
you protest against domestic violence,
you cry when your children are beaten to death,
you shake your head when he can't "do it",
witchcraft you call it, erectile dysfunction or depression,
like ostriches, burying our heads in the sand,
we imagine, if we do nothing it will work out okey,
our actions and lack of actions, create a future.......

So what? you ask,

29 - What They Never Taught Me

What they never taught me....................

The beginning of knowledge,
that which existed before books,
books, a modern invention,
lost is the old knowledge,
handed down from mouth to mouth,

Old knowledge......
from generation to generation,
ancestors from millions of years,
lost, is the value of the knowledge,
of the spirit, of nature........

"It's what my mama taught me"
she learnt from her mother,
and grandmother before her,
learnt from the village elder,
her great great great aunt.

We need references, they say,
we need scientific validation,
mama never used a pen or paper,
it was all in the daily life,
does that make her less of an expert?

Science, academic validation,
aren't we the fancy paperwork generation!?
mama would have laughed,
let them waste time on their toys,
'get back to work child!' she would say

Mama,
villagers depended on her,
now me,
a walking encyclopedia,
as the modernists define it

Cancer, a disease like what Ola had,
the cure took half a year,
a heavy grind, but it paid,
thanks to the plant spirits,
which used to be plenty,

HIV, is that a new virus?
these fancy medical terms!
I had no modern schooling,
medicine is my life, my heritage,
the plants are my pharmacy,

My role?
mother, wife, cook, housekeeper, farmer,
to my village, a medicine expert,
similar knowledge is amiss,
the impacts of modern inventions,

To practice, you must have a degree,
now they say,
me, a descendant of the medicine women?
me, who is paid in milk, vegetables and chicken?
well, I can't afford this 'modern' education,

I sigh as I go along my daily tasks,
mother, wife, cook, farmer,
I might have enjoyed discussions with peers,
isolated,
my knowledge remains untaught,

Except for my daughters,
and maybe their daughters, maybe....
the cycle of relative poverty,
knowledge,
frozen, undermined, and eventually.... lost,

What they never taught me.....

30 - With Every God's Creation

With every god's creation there is a purpose,
whatever that may be.

Just as a farmer plants maize to harvest maize,
just as we paint white, for a white wall,
just as we drink water to quench thirst,
just as we shop for warm cloths against the cold,
with every god's creation there is a purpose.

When he made women and men, it was for a purpose,
giraffes are made with long necks,
elephants with extended trumpets,
monkeys can spring from tree to tree,
and donkeys work without a fee!

When you can't fly as lightly as a bee,
or understand a foreign language,
when you can't win the Olympics,
or capture the heart of a certain guy,
know God has a purpose for you.

Oxygen, carbon dioxide and other gasses,
soil bacteria, sea species, forest species or other,
different characters, different talents and all diversity,
with every god's creation there is a purpose,
whatever that may be.

31 - Character Is Your True Friend

Character is your true friend.
one has to treat it well,
as youth becomes history,
leaving behind bones and wrinkles,
only character remains faithful,
and grow more beautiful with age.

Character is your true friend,
one that needs nurturing,
one day gone is a day too many,
lessons not learnt usually lead to regret,
for as we grow older in time,
learning opportunities may not be given.

Character is your true friend,
the one who will stay forever,
to get you through hard times,
to help a stranger in need,
to teach by example,
to inspire kind deeds,

Character is your true friend,
the one who learns and endures with you,
growing stronger by honest nurturing,
unlike physical beauty,
a fickle friend, fleeing at a sign of sickness,
shuddering at your ageing face...

32 - I Feel The Pain Of The Future

I feel the pain of the future,
the results of what is today,
for the young adults,
the orphans of today,
even as a young woman,
with family support behind me,
the current future has been tough,
many challenges have been met,
but with a roof over my head,
and a warm meal in my belly.

Many times I was tempted to give up,
there are times I almost did,
from a broken heart or two,
those milestones while growing up,
how I persevered some situations,
remains a mystery to-date,
it wasn't for the optimism of my future,
more for the sake of others,
those who cannot stand,
those who have no voice.

I feel the pain of the future,
the results of what is today,
for the many young orphans,
with no family to turn to,
with no chance of high education,
with no safety nets to catch them,
with no marketable skills,

with no support from society,
what is then is in store for them?
can we help create their sustainable future?

So much unnecessary pain.....

33 - God, The Greatest Artist Of All

God, the greatest artist of all,
did he not create the world?
the various creatures of the earth,
the beautiful landscapes,
unlimited water bodies,
the forbidding mountains,
and all the enriching beauty around us?

Yet even as an artists,
his work is not invulnerable,
just as a famous paint will lose value,
if the work is left in rain,
a wood carving may lose value,
if broken from a fall,
such are the limitations of artists,

God, the greatest artist of all,
created mankind as his great art,
not only did he give man life,
brains and intellect to conquer,
he gave him the gift of creation,
vision and talent to create.
so enthusiastic was the great artist,

Man, the next great artist,
creating machines for 'easyfication'
tampering with viruses unknown,
experimenting with bombs to kill,
crossing genes between creations,
vandalism of natural art!
why? Really... why??

God, the greatest artist of all.

34 - All For Fashion, Fashion, Fashion

All for fashion, fashion, fashion,
the stealth master of destruction,
rayon, viscose, modal,
all made from trees,
massive forests destruction,
trees, for food and shelter,
slashed for fashion construction,
we wonder how disaster strikes?
treeless where there used to be trees,
for shelter, food, reproduction, medicine,
for carbon captures,
now with weather elements contribution,
climate change disruptions,
food chains disruptions,
impacts of changes,
direct, indirect,
extinction, one specie then another,
global calamity,
unexpected volcanic eruptions,
hurricanes more often than ever,
extended draught seasons,
sea cyclones making land inhabitable,
changed weather patterns,
all for fashion, fashion, fashion
the stealth master of destruction.

35 - Ten Cents!

Ten cents!
for this dress I sell,
I am a farmer with a family,
for the seedlings we bought,
for the plantation we work on,
and for the harvesting we do,

Ten cents!
for the carting horses we rented,
for the processing we made,
for the tailor downtown,
for the 10 hours he put into,
for the style he thought,

Ten cents!
for all the water being used,
for all the labor incurred,
for all the land degradation,
for the ecosystems destroyed,
for emissions being caused,

Ten cents!
for food,
for insurance,
for school,
for shelter,
for fun,

A hundred euros,
for the dress I buy,
for the brand label added....

36 - Just One More Bucket

Just one more bucket!
she says with a smile,
carrying another bucket of sand from the dry river bed,
their family livelihood,
the developers dream,
a bucket of sand for 50 shillings,
to build someone's house,
yet a sweet or a soda drink,
costs four times as much,
a bucket of sand to pay for education,
how many buckets will that be?
a bucket of sand for food and shelter,
a bucket of sand for feminine needs,
and you better not be sick a day,
several buckets of sand for hospital bills,
just one more bucket,
my little friend says,
she smiles,
I can't do the same,
it is too sad,
I also feel angry,
at the unfairness of poverty,
'just one more bucket', she says,
wasting her childhood away,
cheerfully unaware............
and what costs to the environment?

37 - The Last

The last,
pyrenean ibex,
sabre-toothed cat,
wooly mammoth,
the last,

The last,
passenger pigeon,
dodo,
great auk,
the last.

The last,
he presses the gun, BANG!
a trophy,
that was it for the pyrenean ibex.
the last,

The last,
a magnificent sabre-cat,
in the deepness of the forest,
a hunter's dream,
lonely, wounded, welcoming death.

The last,
wooly mammoth,
taking his final journey,
a marketable fur,
ambushed for the popular fashion.

The last,
passanger pigeon,

lovely and compliant,
no mate, no children,
a lonely death in captivity.

The last,
flightless slow moving dodo,
easy to catch and so delicious,
for the drunken sailor,
the last eggs, a cure for a hangover.

The last,
elegant moving great auk,
delicious, filling and easy prey,
with feathers to trim the finest coats,
a quick death by the hunter's pistol.

The last,
the last,
the last,
always,
the last.....

38 - Racing For The Last Fish

Racing for the last fish,
caught up in the moment.....

Why the race really?
why catch the last fish?
is it for lack of alternatives?
is it for winning a competition?
is it for a collection?
is it for a basic need?

Either way, we race,
we race for the last fish,
be it the last of it's race,
be it the last of the species,
be it for sport,
be it for a basic need,

Racing for the last fish,
caught up in the moment,
this time, it is really the last.......
so what comes next?
could we have done differently?
are we able to change?

39 - All Is Gone

All is gone!
shocked, saddened,
was my reaction,
all that I knew and loved,
all that I called home,
all that I could have gone back to,
all that I could have stood up for,
gone....

All gone............
no more trees to climb,
no zambarau, no sugarcanes,
no oranges, no mangoes,
no cashewnuts or pinapples,
no tamarindes, no guavas,
no mandarines, no mabungo,
childhood memories, all gone.....

....Beautiful houses,
wonderful pollution everywhere,
numerous automobiles,
increased population, gated,
none of the poor indigenous,
an urban feeling.....
no clean water,
not a patch of green!

Gone....
all gone......
it breaks my heart.....

40 - Just Weighing The Scales

Gold industries for the economic development?
just weighing the scales.....

Water depletion,
dying trees,
species extinction,
landscapes destruction,
toxic waste dumps,
cyanide, mercury, arsenic leaching,
hazardous contamination,
air, water, land pollution,
bioaccumulation,
health deterioration,
brain damage, neurological damage, cancer,
skin ulcers, miscarriage, death
hundreds of years with the impacts,
hundred generations with varying disabilities,
or just not born....
just weighing the scales!

No health care,
economic priorities!

No compensation,
economic priorities!

No voice,
economic priorities!

No choice,
economic priorities!

Economic priorities!
economic priorities!
economic priorities!
economic priorities!
gold industries for the economic development?
off course! they always say,
no need to think of other costs,
just losing a few generations?
apparently we can afford it,

41 - The Hypocrisy Of World Organizations

The hypocrisy of world organizations,
a tragedy of the commons, or a global tragedy?
have we fallen so far,
that we can't see the light?
make more money, pay more taxes,
subsidies, grants, loans,
invest! invest! invest!
make more profit,
meet the bottom line,
here, abroad, the moon, anywhere,
nothing is impossible....
ecological footprint?
that's not our concern.

Go! go! go!
the free market is there,
no trade barriers,
they signed the WTO agreement,
no regulations!
they don't have the capacity,
no restrictions!
we saw to that,
pardoning debts,
investor friendly policies,
some expatriates helps well,
global exploitation?
no, we call it competition.

Go! go! go!
take it all,

we are the drivers of globalization,
winning is a must!
we, the world giants,
WTO, IMF, World bank,
we are great at what we do,
we strategize, we get results,
one way or another,
climate change?
that's another department,
we 'invest', we profit, we create poverty issues,
we give strategic grants,
to help them of course,
...... to help ourselves some more,

The ecological footprint?
that's for another organization ....

The hypocrisy of world organizations,
a tragedy of the commons, or a global tragedy?

42 - The Different Shades Of Green

The different shades of green,
and how we color sustainability,

Light green, dark green,
deep green, lime green,

Bright green, neon green,
the different shades of green

Bright green technology,
solar power and biofuels,

Light green shades,
limitation, minimization,

Deep green message,
protect earth, protect species,

Dark green speaks of,
consume green products,

Lime green and neon,
eat green, travel green,

Think whether you are green or not,
and are you all shades of green?

Sustainability commercialized,
with different shades of green......

43 - A New Perspective For The Future

A new perspective for the future,
yes, that is what we need,
starting with our education,
few questions have to be addressed......

Is it applicable in our environment?
the basic needs are indicators,
for all within the society,
does it add value to a life?
to health, shelter and meals?
to happiness, peace, humanity?
to social networks sustainability?
to environmental health and morality?
to resource management possibilities?
to harmony and safety?
to peace and unity?
to fair governance politics?
to inclusive policies?
to empowerment of future generations?

A new perspective for the future,
yes, that is what we need,
starting with our education,
few questions have to be addressed......

44 - My Beloved Great Great Great Great Great Grandchild

My beloved great great great great great grandchild,
this is a generational letter from me to you,
I have loved you before your were here,
you are the reason I do my part,
the year of writing this message is 2019,
to ensure the message is received,
I need to do my part,
to contribute to global sustainability,
for my beloved great great great great great great grand
children,
and more to come......

The challenges are many,
climate change issues causing destruction,
communication tragedies causing war,
we must keep doing our part to ensure survival,
and always leave a generational letter....

My beloved great great great great great grandchild,
this is a generational letter from me to you,
I have loved you before you were here,
you are the reason I do my part,
the year of writing this message is 2019,
to ensure the message is received,
you need to do your part,
to contribute to world sustainability,
for our beloved great great great great great great
grandchildren,
and more to come.......

45 - Are Human Lives A Currency For Development?

Are human lives a currency for development?
how far have we fallen???

Are human lives a currency for development?
for developing countries that is,
where human lives don't seem to matter,
as long as authoritarian leaders keep their seats,
as long as multilateral agreements are signed,
as long as humongous grants are given,
as long as leaders perform in own terms,
what we need is justice, not for one but for all,

Are human lives the currency for development?
I chose to look at mining sectors,
mercury, arsenic and cyanide pollution,
resulting deaths and health disorders,
children falling and dying in open pits,
shootings of any who comes for a peek,
gold contributes to economic development .... or so they say,
investors first, human lives be damned,

Are human lives the currency for development?
legal grants for infrastructures expansions,
illegal demolition of citizens houses,
inconsideration for mother and child,
government induced homelessness,
education disruption, stress, rape, malaria,
no compensation, no safety nets,
infrastructures development, at the cost of human lives?

Are human lives the currency for development?

46 - Sustainable Development, What Else?

Sustainable development is:
"development that meets the needs of the present,
without compromising the abilities of future generations,
to meet their own needs", **Brundtland,1987**
what else....................................?

If the policies you make today,
pollute the oceans or the land away,
that is not sustainable development.

If policies are adopted today,
and cause more poverty than before,
that is not sustainable development.

If free trade brings riches somewhere,
while destroying economies elsewhere,
that is not sustainable development.

If an education syllabus is irrelevant,
neither applicable, efficient nor effective,
that is not sustainable development.

If solutions work in some nations,
yet cause disasters at other nations,
that is not sustainable development.

If a nation's GDP increases from growing industries,
leaving land and lakes unproductive or toxic,
that is not sustainable development.

If policies or punishments hinder girls education,
prematurely incapacitating future generations,
that is not sustainable development.

If individual rights are in any way abused,
emotionally or physically harming a group or person,
that is not sustainable development

Building hydroelectric power plants,
while causing deforestation and species extinction,
that is not sustainable development

Investing in palm oil plantations for biofuels,
causing food chain disruptions and species extinction,
that is not sustainable development

GMO companies claiming to cure world hunger,
while killing soil bacteria and destroying soil quality,
that is not sustainable development

Sustainable development is
*"development that meets the needs of the present,
without compromising the abilities of future generations,
to meet their own needs"*, **Brundtland,1987**

What else....................................?

47 - Thy Name Is True Love

'Thy name is true love....'
an apt name as it turned out,
one that raises much contemplation,
offering no easy solutions.......

Now strolling down the memory lane,
to the day the rascal was born,
bold from the very beginning,
..... and always elusive..........

Whom? that you may well ask,
let's just call him love,
true love may be a better fit,
always worth aspiring for.....

True love, he dreamt the days away,
planning the next grand "gesture"
it has to fit with the vision he sees,
true love, the ultimate prize....

Difficult to describe,
achievement is challenging,
impossible to bribe,
tempting and worth aspiring,

True love, no standard definition,
how then he wonders, can he tell what is real?
what then should the end product look like?
how then should the end product make us feel?

Warm and fuzzy as a love poetry definition?
filled with food and drink perhaps?

days of laughter and endless leisure?
or maybe customized riches as pleased?

If he owns half the world riches,
if he shares it equally with him or her,
if he owns a food factory, and give half to her?
if that is the definition of true love, is it his or hers?

What if owning such riches is not her custom?
what if eating such food is taboo?
is it then the true love of her preference?
what does this mean to you and to her?

'Sustainable development,
thy name is true love......'
a bold concept,
..... and always elusive..........

48 - The Silent Screams

The silent screams,
you can hear them everywhere,
if you close your ears,
and listen................

The silent screams, of desperation
the silent screams of terror,
and those responsible for the situation,
are heaped with honourable titles,

The screams, from a child dying in agony,
cyanide water pollution, from neighbourhood mines,

The screams, from a girl child genital mutilation,
a mother's heartbreak, a father's right,

The screams, of the neighbour's albino child,
his hand for 50 dollars, a leg costs twice as much,

The screams, of an old woman's heartbreak,
a house demolished, for a road expansion project,

The screams, from a mere school child,
abuse of power, a teacher's right,

The screams, of a woman violently abused,
for being late at a market, for not cooking his favourite,

The screams, from the household maid,
from being beaten by the boss, from sexual abuse,

The screams, from children losing a father,
for daring to speak up, of top down corruption,

The screams, from a burning home,
for opposing the ruling power, for speaking up,

The silent screams of desperation,
the silent screams of terror,
and those responsible for the situation,
are heaped with honourable titles,

The silent screams,
you can hear them everywhere,
if you close your ears,
and listen..................

49 - Is This A Practical Joke?

'Child labour must be stopped!', they say,
'the policy is in place', they say,
'the children are protected',
they say.............
the child listens as he must.

'No more work shall you do,
no more manual labour for you,
and if they force you to do it,
you have the right to quit,'
a smile, a few sweets are given to the child.....

'You shall not collect sand for builders,
you shall not work in the farm,
as for those manufacturing factories,
that is no place for a child!'
a satisfactory conclusion, a pat on the head....

'You shall not work in the mines,
nor shall you sale nuts on the streets,
you have the right to play I say,
to go to school and learn,'
a hug, and more hugs...

'One day you will be a teacher,
or maybe even a doctor,
you may want to become an artist,
or be a business director,'
more sweets, a final embrace....

'Aren't they nice?' he muses,
as the development workers wave and left,

'no more manual labour for me,
what about food and shelter payments?
do I then get that for free?'

And what about my little sisters:
what of little Salem's medical costs,
with deadline for payments?
I may be 10 or maybe 13,
but this is my life, not your dream

I am the man of the family,
for my little sisters and brother,
no more child labour? no more legal pay?
is this good for those like us?
child rights? am the child or are you?

Is this a practical joke?

50 - Completion Or Depletion?

Development as a vision,
where does it end?
how does it end?
does it end with....
with completion or depletion?

Practicing development,
or conserving the environment?
completion or depletion?
I ask....

Completion or depletion?
completion or depletion?
completion or depletion?
I ask...

Infrastructures development,
hydroelectric plants,
completion or depletion?
I ask...

Solar panels creation,
monoculture plantations,
completion or depletion?
I ask...

Completion or depletion?
completion or depletion?
completion or depletion?
neither, either or both?
I ask...

51 - Walking Down The Beach

A poem by Niek de Blok

Walking down the beach,
the peace just got disturbed,
I see a big splash in the ocean,
after hearing a big bang,

It is fishermen at work
why are they using dynamite?
why do they feel it's all right?
causing fish genocide?

Are they so desperate for a catch.
that they do not mind blowing up the corals?
do they go home without regrets,
after causing sea life horrors?

Or do they argue with themselves,
wishing there were different ways?
to not destroy the ocean,
yet still come home with decent pay?

Every year the fish are less,
until it really is too late,
no fish left for the nets to catch,
an empty sea, an empty plate....

52 - The Sands Of Time

In the times when ice covered the land,
the world was by different species fanned,
the wooly mammoths were then present,
the short faced bear, the dire wolf,
ground sloths, beautiful armadillos,
saber-toothed cats, giant beavers,
stag-moose, american mastodon,
short-faced skunk,
the famous band of the now extinct,

Earth temperatures continue to raise,
the continuous warming up of the planet,
we now call it global warming,
commercialising with the catchy phrase,
ice melting in the artic,
increased sandstorms in the desert,
prolonged draught in other places,
earthquakes where there never was.
we read the news with detachment.

Climate change is personalised,
it affects all, in different ways,
some ice age species do still exist,
they simply underwent evolution,
biological adjusted to the changes,
elephants, bison and musk ox,
jaguars, porcupines and voles,
horses, cows and sheep,
and even the that rats we despise.

We tend to commercialise climate change,
how else will we sell the news?

how else can we justify adaptation projects?
how else could we justify biofuel plantations?
or deforestation for big dams projects?
how else could we justify mining,
for the minerals to make solar panels?
how else could we justify,
materials needed for sustainable cars?

Humans,
throughout the centuries,
we survive,
at the expense of all species,
we continue to survive,
we plunder,
we manipulate,
we survive...........
throughout the sands of time,

53 - Hydro-Electricty Versus Sustainability

Hydroelectricity versus sustainability,
let us explore without hostility,
water energy is cleaner than coal,
can be setup with a goal,
here or there it does not matter,
although decisions must be smarter,
a natural energy from hydrological cycle,
can be a risk when the weather is fickle.
reservoirs can offer recreation activities,
swimming, fishing, boating and such,
can be used as energy source,
and also as a water source....

Hydroelectricity versus sustainability,
let us explore with agility,
environmental damages cannot be ignored,
even when benefits are being scored,
with natural water flows interrupted,
ecosystems shall be disrupted,
the pollution...is horrendous,
from the first stage to end of process,
land clearance and making roads,
causing biodiversity loss,
land, water and air pollution,
already high on this first stage...

Hydroelectricity versus sustainability,
the question does not bring tranquility,
those who are in power,
seem to be blind from reality...

just look from each operational activity,
those impacts will not bring stability,
we claim it is good for the social-economic,
but that is not the actual reality,
what about greenhouse gasses emissions?
what about displacement costs?
what about associated disasters?
what about food chains and biodiversity loss?

Hydroelectricity versus sustainability,
how do we maintain our sanity?

54 - Remote Work

Remote work ...why not?
if a job can be done from home,
it should be done from home,
isn't this the 21st century?
isn't this the age of technology?
do we not care for the environment?
do we not know the benefits of sleep?
do we not want to improve our health?
and to have a work-life balance?

Remote work ...why not?
it exists for some if not for all,
more can be done with a purpose,
to reduce emissions from transportation,
to improve the health of those affected,
to create opportunities for those segregated,
to reduce the social economic gap,
to retain employees and improve competitiveness,
to allow better employer employee matching...

Remote work ..... a healthy change of business practice,
a mother should not have to choose,
between a job and the children....
a father should not always be tired,
at the end of each day ...
a disabled should be able to work,
at the comfort of their homes ....
those with low immunity should be able to work,
without risk of opportunistic infections...

Remote work ... could we overcome the barriers?
those physical and non physical?

implementation of supporting policies?
proper employees training?
relevant software maybe?
higher speed internet?
building trust with employees?
improving communication?
strengthening sustainability?
remote work ...why not?

If a job can be done from home,
it should be done from home,
isn't this the 21st century?
isn't this the age of technology?
do we not care for the environment?
do we not know the benefits of sleep?
do we not want to improve our health?
and to have a work-life balance?

55 - Are We On The Same Page?

About sustainable development,
are we on the same page?
we internationally make agreements,
without considering local contexts,
while local governments make decsions,
without referring to international agreements,
how do we stay on the same page?
are we willing to make changes?

Governments...
the only potential implementing partners?
I think not.
what about local businesses?
is it time to empower their role?
could a partnership with a business,
ensure employment for women, child right,
and environmental sustainability?

About sustainable development,
are we on the same page?
is it time for new partners?
is it time to empower organizations?
is it time for organizations to implement change?
is it time for employees,
to influence policies?
to bring the change we need?

What if organizations are empowered,
with technology transfer,
with financial investment,
with experienced professionals,
with competitive product designers,

with sustainable supply chains,
with global markets?
could that strengthen sustainability?

What if such organizations comply,
with environmental standards,
with women empowerment,
with humanitarian law,
with products standards,
with participatory decision making,
with international agreements,
would they not make the best partners?

Talking about sustainable development,
can we be on the same page?
maybe by making new partnerships?
or changing the system?
we should use the vision off course,
but we can look at local aims,
and then align objectives,
and create new strategies

Sustainability is a priority,
are we on the same page?

The End

CPSIA information can be obtained
at www.ICGtesting.com
Printed in the USA
BVHW030515051119
562941BV00001B/19/P